10 steps to start your business

INTRODUCTION

Starting a business involves planning, making key financial decisions, and completing a series of legal activities. Scroll down to learn about each step.

Table Of Contents

Heading 1. Conduct market research

Heading 2. Write your business plan

Heading 3. Fund your business

Heading 4. Pick your business location

Heading 5. Choose a business structure

Heading 6. Choose your business name

Heading 7. Register your business

Heading 8. Get federal and state tax IDs

Heading 9. Apply for licenses and permits

Heading 10. Open a business bank account

Conduct market research

Market research will tell you if there's an opportunity to turn your idea into a successful business. It's a way to gather information about potential customers and businesses already operating in your area. Use that information to find a competitive advantage for your business.

Market research and competitive analysis

Market research helps you find customers for your business. Competitive analysis helps you make your business unique. Combine them to find a competitive advantage for your small business.

- Use market research to find customers

Market research blends consumer behavior and economic trends to confirm and improve your business idea.

It's crucial to understand your consumer base from the outset. Market research lets you reduce risks even while your business is still just a gleam in your eye.

Gather demographic information to better understand opportunities and limitations for gaining customers. This could include population data on age, wealth, family, interests, or anything else that's relevant for your business.

Then answer the following questions to get a good sense of your market:

Demand: Is there a desire for your product or service?
Market size: How many people would be interested in your offering?
Economic indicators: What is the income range and employment rate?
Location: Where do your customers live and where can your business reach?
Market saturation: How many similar options are already available to consumers?
Pricing: What do potential customers pay for these alternatives?

You'll also want to keep up with the latest small business trends. It's important to gain a sense of the specific market share that will impact your profits.

You can do market research using existing sources, or you can do the research yourself and go direct to consumers.

Existing sources can save you a lot of time and energy, but the information might not be as specific to your audience as you'd like. Use it to answer questions that are both general and quantifiable, like industry trends, demographics, and household incomes. Check online to see more results on that.

Asking consumers yourself can give you a nuanced understanding of your specific target audience. But, direct research can be time consuming and expensive. Use it to answer questions about your specific business or customers, like reactions to your logo, improvements you could make to buying experience, and where customers might go instead of your business.

Here are a few methods you can use to do direct research:

- Surveys
- Questionnaires
- Focus groups
- In-depth interviews

Use competitive analysis to find a market advantage

Competitive analysis helps you learn from businesses competing for your potential customers. This is key to defining a competitive edge that creates sustainable revenue.

Your competitive analysis should identify your competition by product line or service and market segment. Assess the following characteristics of the competitive landscape:

- Market share

- Strengths and weaknesses
- Your window of opportunity to enter the market
- The importance of your target market to your competitors
- Any barriers that may hinder you as you enter the market
- Indirect or secondary competitors who may impact your success

Several industries might be competing to serve the same market you're targeting. The Department of Justice provides a diagram of Porter's Five Forces as one way you can differentiate your competitive analysis by industry. Important factors to consider include level of competition, threat of new competitors or services, and the effect of suppliers and customers on price.

Free small business data and trends
There are many reliable sources that provide customer and market information at no cost. Free statistics are readily available to help prospective small business owners.

Write your business plan

Your business plan is the foundation of your business. It's a roadmap for how to structure, run, and grow your new business. You'll use it to convince people that working with you — or investing in your company — is a smart choice.

Business plans help you run your business

A good business plan guides you through each stage of starting and managing your business. You'll use your business plan as a roadmap for how to structure, run, and grow your new business. It's a way to think through the key elements of your business.

Business plans can help you get funding or bring on new business partners. Investors want to feel confident they'll see a return on their investment. Your business plan is the tool you'll use to convince people that working with you — or investing in your company — is a smart choice.

Pick a business plan format that works for you

There's no right or wrong way to write a business plan. What's important is that your plan meets your needs.

Most business plans fall into one of two common categories: traditional or lean startup.

Traditional business plans are more common, use a standard structure, and encourage you to go into detail in each section. They tend to require more work upfront and can be dozens of pages long.

Lean startup business plans are less common but still use a standard structure. They focus on summarizing only the most important points of the key elements of your plan. They can take as little as one hour to make and are typically only one page.

Traditional business plan
This type of plan is very detailed, takes more time to write, and is comprehensive. Lenders and investors commonly request this plan.

Lean startup plan
This type of plan is high-level focus, fast to write, and contains key elements only. Some lenders and investors may ask for more information.

Traditional business plan format

You might prefer a traditional business plan format if you're very detail-oriented, want a comprehensive plan, or plan to request financing from traditional sources.

When you write your business plan, you don't have to stick to the exact business plan outline. Instead, use the sections that make the most sense for your business and your needs. Traditional business plans use some combination of these nine sections.

Executive summary
Briefly tell your reader what your company is and why it will be successful. Include your mission statement, your product or service, and basic information about your company's leadership team, employees, and location. You should also include financial information and high-level growth plans if you plan to ask for financing.

Company description
Use your company description to provide detailed information about your company. Go into detail about the problems your business solves. Be specific, and list out the consumers, organization, or businesses your company plans to serve.

Explain the competitive advantages that will make your business a success. Are there experts on your team? Have you found the perfect location for your store? Your company description is the place to boast about your strengths.
Market analysis

You'll need a good understanding of your industry outlook and target market. Competitive research will show you what other businesses are doing and what their strengths are. In your market research, look for trends and themes. What do successful competitors do? Why does it work? Can you do it better? Now's the time to answer these questions.

Organization and management

Tell your reader how your company will be structured and who will run it.

Describe the legal structure of your business. State whether you have or intend to incorporate your business as a C or an S corporation, form a general or limited partnership, or if you're a sole proprietor or limited liability company (LLC).

Use an organizational chart to lay out who's in charge of what in your company. Show how each person's unique experience will contribute to the success of your venture. Consider including resumes and CVs of key members of your team.

Service or product line

Describe what you sell or what service you offer. Explain how it benefits your customers and what the product lifecycle looks like. Share your plans for intellectual property, like copyright or patent filings. If you're doing research and development for your service or product, explain it in detail.

Marketing and sales

There's no single way to approach a marketing strategy. Your strategy should evolve and change to fit your unique needs.

Your goal in this section is to describe how you'll attract and retain customers. You'll also describe how a sale will actually happen. You'll refer to this section later when you make financial projections, so make sure to thoroughly describe your complete marketing and sales strategies.

Funding request

If you're asking for funding, this is where you'll outline your funding requirements. Your goal is to clearly explain how much funding you'll need over the next five years and what you'll use it for.

Specify whether you want debt or equity, the terms you'd like applied, and the length of time your request will cover. Give a detailed description of how you'll use your funds. Specify if you need funds to buy equipment or materials, pay salaries, or cover specific bills until revenue increases. Always include a description of your future strategic financial plans, like paying off debt or selling your business.

Financial projections

Supplement your funding request with financial projections. Your goal is to convince the reader that your business is stable and will be a financial success.

If your business is already established, include income statements, balance sheets, and cash flow statements for the last three to five years. If you have other collateral you could put against a loan, make sure to list it now.

Provide a prospective financial outlook for the next five years. Include forecasted income statements, balance sheets, cash flow statements, and capital expenditure budgets. For the first year, be even more specific and use quarterly — or even monthly — projections. Make sure to clearly explain your projections, and match them to your funding requests.

This is a great place to use graphs and charts to tell the financial story of your business.

Appendix

Use your appendix to provide supporting documents or other materials were specially requested. Common items to include are credit histories, resumes, product pictures, letters of reference, licenses, permits, patents, legal documents, and other contracts.

Lean startup format

You might prefer a lean startup format if you want to explain or start your business quickly, your business is relatively simple, or you plan to regularly change and refine your business plan.

Lean startup formats are charts that use only a handful of elements to describe your company's value proposition, infrastructure, customers, and finances. They're useful for visualizing tradeoffs and fundamental facts about your company.

There are different ways to develop a lean startup template. You can search the web to find free templates to build your business plan. We discuss nine components of a model business plan here:

Key partnerships

Note the other businesses or services you'll work with to run your business. Think about suppliers, manufacturers, subcontractors, and similar strategic partners.

Key activities

List the ways your business will gain a competitive advantage. Highlight things like selling direct to consumers, or using technology to tap into the sharing economy.

Key resources

List any resource you'll leverage to create value for your customer. Your most important assets could include staff, capital, or intellectual property. Don't forget to leverage business resources that might be available to women, veterans, Native Americans, and HUBZone businesses.

Value proposition

Make a clear and compelling statement about the unique value your company brings to the market.

Customer relationships

Describe how customers will interact with your business. Is it automated or personal? In person or online? Think through the customer experience from start to finish.

Customer segments

Be specific when you name your target market. Your business won't be for everybody, so it's important to have a clear sense of whom your business will serve.

Channels

List the most important ways you'll talk to your customers. Most businesses use a mix of channels and optimize them over time.

Cost structure

Will your company focus on reducing cost or maximizing value? Define your strategy, then list the most significant costs you'll face pursuing it.

Revenue streams
Explain how your company will actually make money.
Some examples are direct sales, memberships fees,
and selling advertising space. If your company has
multiple revenue streams, list them all.

Fund your business

Your business plan will help you figure out how much money you'll need to start your business. If you don't have that amount on hand, you'll need to either raise or borrow the capital. Fortunately, there are more ways than ever to find the capital you need.

Fund your business
It costs money to start a business. Funding your business is one of the first — and most important — financial choices most business owners make. How you choose to fund your business could affect how you structure and run your business.

Determine how much funding you'll need

Every business has different needs, and no financial solution is one-size-fits-all. Your personal financial situation and vision for your business will shape the financial future of your business.

Once you know how much startup funding you'll need, it's time to figure out how you'll get it.

there are three (3) major ways to fund your business which I listed below.

- Self-funding
- Investors

- Loans

Fund your business yourself with self-funding

Otherwise known as bootstrapping, self-funding lets you leverage your own financial resources to support your business. Self-funding can come in the form of turning to family and friends for capital, using your savings accounts, or even tapping into your 401(k).

With self-funding, you retain complete control over the business, but you also take on all the risk yourself. Be careful not to spend more than you can afford, and be especially careful if you choose to tap into retirement accounts early. You might face expensive fees or penalties, or damage your ability to retire on time — so you should check with your plan's administrator and a personal financial advisor first.

Get venture capital from investors

Investors can give you funding to start your business in the form of venture capital investments. Venture capital is normally offered in exchange for an ownership share and active role in the company.

Venture capital differs from traditional financing in a number of important ways. Venture capital typically

- Focuses high-growth companies
- Invests capital in return for equity, rather than debt (it's not a loan)
- Takes higher risks in exchange for potential higher returns
- Has a longer investment horizon than traditional financing

Almost all venture capitalists will, at a minimum, want a seat on the board of directors. So be prepared to give up some portion of both control and ownership of your company in exchange for funding.

How to get venture capital funding

There's no guaranteed way to get venture capital, but the process generally follows a standard order of basic steps.

Find an investor

Look for individual investors — sometimes called "angel investors" — or venture capital firms. Be sure to do enough background research to know if the investor is reputable and has experience working with startup companies.

Share your business plan

The investor will review your business plan to make sure it meets their investing criteria. Most investment funds concentrate on an industry, geographic area, or stage of business development.

Go through due diligence review

The investors will look at your company's management team, market, products and services, corporate governance documents, and financial statements.

Work out the terms
If they want to invest, the next step is to agree on a term sheet that describes the terms and conditions for the fund to make an investment.

Investment
Once you agree on a term sheet, you can get the investment! Once a venture fund has invested, it becomes actively involved in the company. Venture funds normally come in "rounds." As the company meets milestones, further rounds of financing are made available, with adjustments in price as the company executes its plan.

Use crowdfunding to fund your business

Crowdfunding raises funds for a business from a large number of people, called crowdfunders. Crowdfunders aren't technically investors, because they don't receive a share of ownership in the business and don't expect a financial return on their money.

Instead, crowdfunders expect to get a "gift" from your company as thanks for their contribution. Often, that gift is the product you plan to sell or other special perks, like meeting the business owner or getting their name in the credits. This makes crowdfunding a popular option for people who want to produce creative works (like a documentary), or a physical product (like a high-tech cooler).

Crowdfunding is also popular because it's very low risk for business owners. Not only do you get to retain full control of your company, but if your plan fails, you're typically under no obligation to repay your crowdfunders. Every crowdfunding platform is different, so make sure to read the fine print and understand your full financial and legal obligations.

Small Business Administration

MENU

Back to all topics

Fund your business

It costs money to start a business. Funding your business is one of the first — and most important — financial choices most business owners make. How you choose to fund your business could affect how you structure and run your business.

Content

Determine how much funding you'll need

Fund your business yourself with self-funding

Get venture capital from investors

Use crowdfunding to fund your business

Get a small business loan

Use Lender Match to find lenders who offer SBA-guaranteed loans

SBA investment programs

Determine how much funding you'll need

Every business has different needs, and no financial solution is one-size-fits-all. Your personal financial situation and vision for your business will shape the financial future of your business.

Once you know how much startup funding you'll need, it's time to figure out how you'll get it.

Piggy bank
Self-funding
Man in shirt and tie
Investors
Bank and money
Loans

Fund your business yourself with self-funding
Otherwise known as bootstrapping, self-funding lets you leverage your own financial resources to support your business. Self-funding can come in the form of turning to family and friends for capital, using your savings accounts, or even tapping into your 401(k).

With self-funding, you retain complete control over the business, but you also take on all the risk yourself. Be careful not to spend more than you can afford, and be especially careful if you choose to tap into retirement accounts early. You might face expensive fees or penalties, or damage your ability to retire on time — so you should check with your plan's administrator and a personal financial advisor first.

Get venture capital from investors
Investors can give you funding to start your business in the form of venture capital investments. Venture capital is normally offered in exchange for an ownership share and active role in the company.

Venture capital differs from traditional financing in a number of important ways. Venture capital typically:

Focuses high-growth companies
Invests capital in return for equity, rather than debt (it's not a loan)
Takes higher risks in exchange for potential higher returns

Has a longer investment horizon than traditional financing
Almost all venture capitalists will, at a minimum, want a seat on the board of directors. So be prepared to give up some portion of both control and ownership of your company in exchange for funding.

How to get venture capital funding
There's no guaranteed way to get venture capital, but the process generally follows a standard order of basic steps.

Find an investor

Look for individual investors — sometimes called "angel investors" — or venture capital firms. Be sure to do enough background research to know if the investor is reputable and has experience working with startup companies.

Share your business plan

The investor will review your business plan to make sure it meets their investing criteria. Most investment funds concentrate on an industry, geographic area, or stage of business development.

Go through due diligence review

The investors will look at your company's management team, market, products and services, corporate governance documents, and financial statements.

Work out the terms

If they want to invest, the next step is to agree on a term sheet that describes the terms and conditions for the fund to make an investment.

Investment

Once you agree on a term sheet, you can get the investment! Once a venture fund has invested, it becomes actively involved in the company. Venture funds normally come in "rounds." As the company meets milestones, further rounds of financing are made available, with adjustments in price as the company executes its plan.

No treasure map necessary

When John and Kelly didn't have enough money to open their auto repair shop, they got an SBA-backed loan to help start their business.

Use crowdfunding to fund your business

Crowdfunding raises funds for a business from a large number of people, called crowdfunders. Crowdfunders aren't technically investors, because they don't receive a share of ownership in the business and don't expect a financial return on their money.

Instead, crowdfunders expect to get a "gift" from your company as thanks for their contribution. Often, that gift is the product you plan to sell or other special perks, like meeting the business owner or getting their name in the credits. This makes crowdfunding a popular option for people who want to produce creative works (like a documentary), or a physical product (like a high-tech cooler).

Crowdfunding is also popular because it's very low risk for business owners. Not only do you get to retain full control of your company, but if your plan fails, you're typically under no obligation to repay your crowdfunders. Every crowdfunding platform is different, so make sure to read the fine print and understand your full financial and legal obligations.

Get a small business loan

If you want to retain complete control of your business, but don't have enough funds to start, consider a small business loan.

To increase your chances of securing a loan, you should have a business plan, expense sheet, and financial projections for the next five years. These tools will give you an idea of how much you'll need to ask for, and will help the bank know they're making a smart choice by giving you a loan.

Once you have your materials ready, contact banks and credit unions to request a loan. You'll want to compare offers to get the best possible terms for your loan.

**Use Lender Match to find lenders who offer
SBA-guaranteed loans**

If you have trouble getting a traditional business loan,
you should look into SBA-guaranteed loans. When a
bank thinks your business is too risky to lend money to,
the U.S. Small Business Administration (SBA) can agree
to guarantee your loan. That way, the bank has less risk
and is more willing to give your business a loan.

Use Lender Match to find lenders who offer
SBA-guaranteed loans.

⁷Pick your business location

Your business location is one of the most important decisions you'll make. Whether you're setting up a brick-and-mortar business or launching an online store, the choices you make could affect your taxes, legal requirements, and revenue.

Pick your business location

Your business location determines the taxes, zoning laws, and regulations your business will be subject to. You'll need to make a strategic decision about which state, city, and neighborhood you choose to start your business in.

Research the best place to locate your business

You'll need to register your business, pay taxes, and get licenses and permits in the place you choose to locate your business.

Where you locate your business depends in part on the location of your target market, business partners, and your personal preferences. In addition, you should consider the costs, benefits, and restrictions of different government agencies.

Region-specific business expenses

When you calculate your startup costs, take into account the way different expenses might cost more or less depending on your location.

Costs that can vary significantly by location include standard salaries, minimum wage laws, property values, rental rates, business insurance rates, utilities, and government licenses and fees.

Local zoning ordinances

If you buy, rent, build, or plan to work out of a physical property for your business, make sure it conforms to local zoning requirements.

Neighborhoods are generally zoned for either commercial or residential use. Zoning ordinances can restrict or entirely ban specific kinds of businesses from operating in an area.

You might have fewer zoning restrictions if you base your business out of your home, but zoning ordinances can still apply even to home-based businesses.

Zoning laws are typically controlled at the local level, so check with your department of city planning, or similar office, to find out about the zoning laws in your area.

State and local taxes

Consider the tax landscape for the state, county, and city. Income tax, sales tax, property tax, and corporate taxes can vary significantly from place to place.

In fact, some states are well-known for creating tax environments that are very friendly to certain kinds of companies. That's part of the reason why tech startups, financial institutions, and manufacturing tend to concentrate in certain areas of the country.

Visit state and local government websites to find out what the tax landscape for your area looks like.

State and local government incentives

Some state and local governments offer special tax credits for small businesses. You might also find state-specific small business loans or other financial incentives.

Incentive programs and benefits are often related to job creation, energy efficiency, urban redevelopment, and technology.

Federal government incentives

The federal government offers benefits to small businesses that contract with the government and are based in underutilized areas.

Choose a business structure

The legal structure you choose for your business will impact your business registration requirements, how much you pay in taxes, and your personal liability.

Choose a business structure
The business structure you choose influences everything from day-to-day operations, to taxes and how much of your personal assets are at risk. You should choose a business structure that gives you the right balance of legal protections and benefits.

Your business structure affects how much you pay in taxes, your ability to raise money, the paperwork you need to file, and your personal liability.

You'll need to choose a business structure before you register your business with the state. Most businesses will also need to get a tax ID number and file for the appropriate licenses and permits.

Choose carefully. While you may convert to a different business structure in the future, there may be restrictions based on your location. This could also result in tax consequences and unintended dissolution, among other complications.

Consulting with business counselors, attorneys, and accountants can prove helpful.

Sole proprietorship
A sole proprietorship is easy to form and gives you complete control of your business. You're automatically considered to be a sole proprietorship if you do business activities but don't register as any other kind of business.

Sole proprietorships do not produce a separate business entity. This means your business assets and liabilities are not separate from your personal assets and liabilities. You can be held personally liable for the debts and obligations of the business. Sole proprietors are still able to get a trade name. It can also be hard to raise money because you can't sell stock, and banks are hesitant to lend to sole proprietorships.

Sole proprietorships can be a good choice for low-risk businesses and owners who want to test their business idea before forming a more formal business.

Partnership

Partnerships are the simplest structure for two or more people to own a business together. There are two common kinds of partnerships: limited partnerships (LP) and limited liability partnerships (LLP).

Limited partnerships have only one general partner with unlimited liability, and all other partners have limited liability. The partners with limited liability also tend to have limited control over the company, which is documented in a partnership agreement. Profits are passed through to personal tax returns, and the general partner — the partner without limited liability — must also pay self-employment taxes.

Limited liability partnerships are similar to limited partnerships, but give limited liability to every owner. An LLP protects each partner from debts against the partnership, they won't be responsible for the actions of other partners.

Partnerships can be a good choice for businesses with multiple owners, professional groups (like attorneys), and groups who want to test their business idea before forming a more formal business.

Limited liability company (LLC)

An LLC lets you take advantage of the benefits of both the corporation and partnership business structures.

LLCs protect you from personal liability in most instances, your personal assets — like your vehicle, house, and savings accounts — won't be at risk in case your LLC faces bankruptcy or lawsuits.

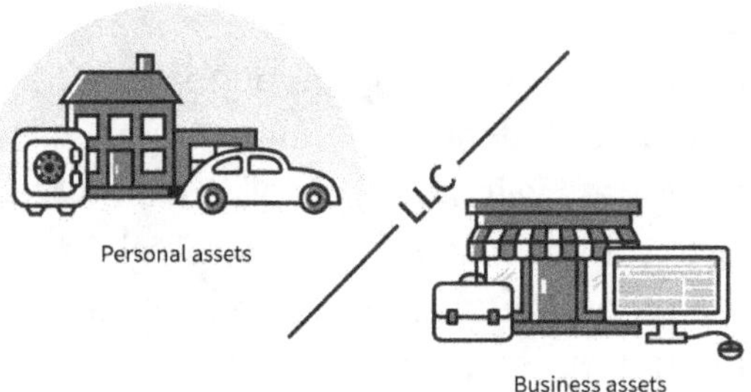

Profits and losses can get passed through to your personal income without facing corporate taxes. However, members of an LLC are considered self-employed and must pay self-employment tax contributions towards Medicare and Social Security.

LLCs can have a limited life in many states. When a member joins or leaves an LLC, some states may require the LLC to be dissolved and re-formed with new membership — unless there's already an agreement in place within the LLC for buying, selling, and transferring ownership.

LLCs can be a good choice for medium- or higher-risk businesses, owners with significant personal assets they want protected, and owners who want to pay a lower tax rate than they would with a corporation.

Corporation

- **C corp**

A corporation, sometimes called a C corp, is a legal entity that's separate from its owners. Corporations can make a profit, be taxed, and can be held legally liable.

Corporations offer the strongest protection to its owners from personal liability, but the cost to form a corporation is higher than other structures. Corporations also require more extensive record-keeping, operational processes, and reporting.

Unlike sole proprietors, partnerships, and LLCs, corporations pay income tax on their profits. In some cases, corporate profits are taxed twice — first, when the company makes a profit, and again when dividends are paid to shareholders on their personal tax returns.

Corporations have a completely independent life separate from its shareholders. If a shareholder leaves the company or sells his or her shares, the C corp can continue doing business relatively undisturbed.

Corporations have an advantage when it comes to raising capital because they can raise funds through the sale of stock, which can also be a benefit in attracting employees.

Corporations can be a good choice for medium- or higher-risk businesses, those that need to raise money, and businesses that plan to "go public" or eventually be sold.

- **S corp**

An S corporation, sometimes called an S corp, is a special type of corporation that's designed to avoid the double taxation drawback of regular C corps. S corps allow profits, and some losses, to be passed through directly to owners' personal income without ever being subject to corporate tax rates.

Not all states tax S corps equally, but most recognize them the same way the federal government does and tax the shareholders accordingly. Some states tax S corps on profits above a specified limit and other states don't recognize the S corp election at all, simply treating the business as a C corp.

S corps must file with the IRS to get S corp status, a different process from registering with their state.

There are special limits on S corps. Check the IRS website for eligibility requirements. You'll still have to follow the strict filing and operational processes of a C corp.

S corps also have an independent life, just like C corps. If a shareholder leaves the company or sells his or her shares, the S corp can continue doing business relatively undisturbed.

S corps can be a good choice for a businesses that would otherwise be a C corp, but meet the criteria to file as an S corp.

- **B corp**

A benefit corporation, sometimes called a B corp, is a for-profit corporation recognized by a majority of U.S. states. B corps are different from C corps in purpose, accountability, and transparency, but aren't different in how they're taxed.

B corps are driven by both mission and profit. Shareholders hold the company accountable to produce some sort of public benefit in addition to a financial profit. Some states require B corps to submit annual benefit reports that demonstrate their contribution to the public good.

There are several third-party B corp certification services, but none are required for a company to be legally considered a B corp in a state where the legal status is available.

Close corporation

Close corporations resemble B corps but have a less traditional corporate structure. These shed many formalities that typically govern corporations and apply to smaller companies.

State rules vary, but shares are usually barred from public trading. Close corporations can be run by a small group of shareholders without a board of directors.

Nonprofit corporation

Nonprofit corporations are organized to do charity, education, religious, literary, or scientific work. Because their work benefits the public, nonprofits can receive tax-exempt status, meaning they don't pay state or federal income taxes on any profits it makes.

Nonprofits must file with the IRS to get tax exemption, a different process from registering with their state.

Nonprofit corporations need to follow organizational rules very similar to a regular C corp. They also need to follow special rules about what they do with any profits they earn. For example, they can't distribute profits to members or political campaigns.

Nonprofits are often called 501(c)(3) corporations — a reference to the section of the Internal Revenue Code that is most commonly used to grant tax-exempt status.

Cooperative

A cooperative is a business or organization owned by and operated for the benefit of those using its services. Profits and earnings generated by the cooperative are distributed among the members, also known as user-owners. Typically, an elected board of directors and officers run the cooperative while regular members have voting power to control the direction of the cooperative. Members can become part of the cooperative by purchasing shares, though the amount of shares they hold does not affect the weight of their vote.

Combine different business structures

Designations like S corp and nonprofit aren't strictly business structures — they can also be understood as a tax status. It's possible for an LLC to be taxed as a C corp, S corp, or a nonprofit. These arrangements are far less common and can be more difficult to set up. If you're considering one of these non-standard structures, you should speak with a business counselor or an attorney to help you decide.

Compare business structures

Compare the general traits of these business structures, but remember that ownership rules, liability, taxes, and filing requirements for each business structure can vary by state. The following table is intended only as a guideline. Please confer with a business tax specialist to confirm your specific business needs.

Business structure	Sole proprietorship
Ownership	One person
Liability	Unlimited personal liability
Taxes	Self-employment tax Personal tax

Business structure	Partnerships
Ownership	Two or more people
Liability	Unlimited personal liability unless structured as a limited partnership
Taxes	Self-employment tax (except for limited partners) Personal tax

Business structure	Limited liability company (LLC)
Ownership	One or more people
Liability	Owners are not personally liable
Taxes	Self-employment tax Personal tax or corporate tax

Business structure	Corporation - C corp
Ownership	One or more people
Liability	Owners are not personally liable
Taxes	Corporate tax

Business structure	Corporation - S corp
Ownership	One or more people, but no more than 100, and all must be U.S. citizens
Liability	Owners are not personally liable
Taxes	Personal tax

Business structure	Corporation - B corp
Ownership	One or more people
Liability	Owners are not personally liable
Taxes	Corporate tax

Business structure	Corporation - Nonprofit
Ownership	One or more people
Liability	Owners are not personally liable
Taxes	Tax-exempt, but corporate profits can't be distributed

Choose your business name

It's not easy to pick the perfect name. You'll want one that reflects your brand and captures your spirit. You'll also want to make sure your business name isn't already being used by someone else.

Choose your business name
You can find the right business name with creativity and market research. Once you've picked your name, you should protect it by registering it with the right agencies.

Register your business name to protect it

You'll want to choose a business name that reflects your brand identity and doesn't clash with the types of goods and services you offer.

Once you settle on a name you like, you need to protect it. There are four different ways to register your business name. Each way of registering your name serves a different purpose, and some may be legally required depending on your business structure and location.

- Entity name protects you at a state level
- Trademark protects you at a federal level
- Doing business as (DBA) doesn't give legal protection, but it might be legally required
- Domain name protects your business website address

Each of these name registrations are legally independent. Most small businesses try to use the same name for each kind of registration, but you're not normally required to.

Four different ways to register your business name

- **Entity name**

An entity name can protect the name of your business at a state level. Depending on your business structure and location, the state may require you to register a legal entity name.

Your entity name is how the state identifies your business. Each state may have different rules about what your entity name can be and usage of company suffixes. Most states don't allow you to register a name that's already been registered by someone else, and some states require your entity name to reflect the kind of business it represents.

In most cases, your entity name registration protects your business and prevents anyone else in the state from operating under the same entity name. However, there are exceptions pertaining to state and business structure.

Check with your state for rules about how to register your business name.

- **Trademark**

A trademark can protect the name of your business, goods, and services at a national level. Trademarks prevent others in the same (or similar) industry in the United States from using your trademarked names.

For example, if you were an electronics company and wanted to call your business Springfield Electronic Accessories and one of your products Screen Cover 5000, trademarking those names would prevent other electronics businesses or similar products from using those same names.

Businesses in every state are subject to trademark infringement lawsuits, which can prove costly. That's why you should check your prospective business, product, and service names against the official trademark database, maintained by the United States Patent and Trademark Office.

- **Doing business as (DBA) name**

You might need to register your DBA — also known as a trade name, fictitious name, or assumed name — with the state, county, or city your business is located in. Registering your DBA name doesn't provide legal protection by itself, but most states require you to register your DBA if you use one. Some business structures require you to use a DBA.

Even if you're not required to register a DBA, you might want to anyway. A DBA lets you conduct business under a different identity from your own personal name or your formal business entity name. As an added bonus, getting a DBA and federal tax ID number (EIN) allows you to open a business bank account.

Multiple businesses can go by the same DBA in one state, so you're less restricted in what you can choose. There's also more leeway in the clarity of business function. For example, a small business owner could use Springfield Electronic Accessories for their entity name but use TechBuddy for their DBA. Just remember that trademark infringement laws will still apply.

Determine your DBA requirements based on your specific location. Requirements vary by business structure as well as by state, county, and municipality, so check with local government offices and websites.

- **Domain name**

If you want an online presence for your business, start by registering a domain name — also known as your website address, or URL.

Once you register your domain name, no one else can use it for as long as you continue to own it. It's a good way to protect your brand presence online.

If someone else has already registered the domain you wanted to use, that's okay. Your domain name doesn't actually need to be the same as your legal business name, trademark, or DBA. For example, Springfield Electronic Accessories could register the domain name techbuddyspringfield.com.

You'll register your domain name through a registrar service. Consult a directory of accredited registrars to determine which ones are safe to use, and then pick one that offers you the best combination of price and customer service. You'll need to renew your domain registration on a regular basis.

Register your business

Once you've picked the perfect business name, it's time to make it legal and protect your brand. If you're doing business under a name different than your own, you'll need to register with the federal government, and maybe your state government, too.

Register your business
Register your business to make it a distinct legal entity. How and where you need to register depends on your business structure and business location.

Find out if you need to register your business

Your location and business structure determine how you'll need to register your business. Determine those factors first, and registration becomes very straightforward.

For most small businesses, registering your business is as simple as registering your business name with state and local governments.

In some cases, you don't need to register at all. If you conduct business as yourself using your legal name, you won't need to register anywhere. But remember, if you don't register your business, you could miss out on personal liability protection, legal benefits, and tax benefits.

Get federal and state tax IDs

You'll use your employer identification number (EIN) for important steps to start and grow your business, like opening a bank account and paying taxes. It's like a social security number for your business. Some — but not all — states require you to get a tax ID as well.

Get federal and state tax ID numbers
Your state tax ID and federal tax ID numbers — also known as an Employer Identification Number (EIN) — work like a personal social security number, but for your business. They let your small business pay state and federal taxes.

Get a federal tax ID number

Your Employer Identification Number (EIN) is your federal tax ID. You need it to pay federal taxes, hire employees, open a bank account, and apply for business licenses and permits.

It's free to apply for an EIN, and you should do it right after you register your business.

Your business needs a federal tax ID number if it does any of the following:

- Pays employees
- Operates as a corporation of partnership

- Files tax returns for employment, excise, or alcohol, tobacco, and firearms
- Withholds taxes on income, other than wages, paid to a non-resident alien
- Uses a Keogh Plan (a tax-deferred pension plan)
- Works with certain types of organizations

Change or replace your EIN

If you already have an EIN, you might have to change or replace it with a new one if certain changes have occurred with your business, depending on your business structure and the kind of change that occurred. Check with the IRS to determine exactly whether you need to change or replace your EIN.

Get a state tax ID number

The need for a state tax ID number ties directly to whether your business must pay state taxes. Sometimes, you can use state tax ID numbers for other functions, like protection against identity theft for sole proprietors.

Tax obligations differ at the state and local levels, so you'll need to check with your state's websites.

To know whether you need a state tax ID, research and understand your state's laws regarding income taxes and employment taxes, the two most common forms of state taxes for small businesses.

The process to get a state tax ID number is similar to getting a federal tax ID number, but it will vary by state. You'll have to check with your state government for specific steps.

State income and employment taxes for businesses

Seven states have no income tax, and another two only impose tax on income from dividends. States that do tax income will determine figures based on business structure.

Taxes also vary by state on employment insurance and workers' compensation insurance. Understand these and other implications in calculating startup costs and choosing a business structure.

Visit your state's website to identify whether you need to get a state tax ID number in order to pay state taxes.

Apply for licenses and permits

Keep your business running smoothly by staying legally compliant. The licenses and permits you need for your business will vary by industry, state, location, and other factors.

Apply for licenses and permits
Most small businesses need a combination of licenses and permits from both federal and state agencies. The requirements — and fees — vary based on your business activities, location, and government rules.

Federal licenses and permits

You'll need to get a federal license or permit if your business activities are regulated by a federal agency.

Check to see if any of your business activities are listed here, and then check with the right federal agency to see how to apply.

Requirements and fees depend on your business activity and the agency issuing the license or permit. It's best to check with the issuing agency for details on the business license cost.

Business activity	Agriculture
Description	If you import or transport animals, animal products, biologics, biotechnology or plants across state line.
Issuing agency	U.S. Department of Agriculture

Business activity	Alcoholic beverages
Description	If you manufacture, wholesale, import, or sell alcoholic beverages at a retail location.
Issuing agency	Alcohol and Tobacco Tax and Trade Bureau Local Alcohol Beverage Control Board

Business activity	Aviation
Description	If your business involves operating aircraft, transporting goods or people via air, or aircraft maintenance.
Issuing agency	Federal Aviation Administration

Business activity	Firearms, ammunition, and explosives
Description	If your business manufactures, deals, or imports firearms, ammunitions, and explosives.
Issuing agency	Bureau of Alcohol, Tobacco, Firearms and Explosives

Business activity	Fish and wildlife
Description	If your business engages in any wildlife related activity, including the import or export of wildlife and derivative products.
Issuing agency	U.S. Fish and Wildlife Service

Business activity	Commercial fisheries
Description	If your business engages in commercial fishing of any kind.
Issuing agency	National Oceanic and Atmospheric Administration Fisheries Service

Business activity	Maritime transportation
Description	If you provide ocean transportation or facilitate the shipment of cargo by sea.
Issuing agency	Federal Maritime Commission

Business activity	Mining and drilling
Description	If your business is involved in drilling for natural gas, oil, or other mineral resources on federal lands.
Issuing agency	Bureau of Safety and Environmental Enforcement

Business activity	Nuclear energy
Description	If your business produces commercial nuclear energy, is a fuel cycle facility, or is involved in distribution and disposal of nuclear materials.
Issuing agency	U.S. Nuclear Regulatory Commission

Business activity	Radio and television broadcasting
Description	If your business broadcasts information by radio, television, wire, satellite, or cable.
Issuing agency	Federal Communications Commission

Business activity	Transportation and logistics
Description	If your business operates an oversize or overweight vehicle. Permits for oversize and overweight vehicles are issued by your state government, but the U.S. Department of Transportation can direct you to the correct state office.
Issuing agency	U.S. Department of Transportation

State licenses and permits

The licenses and permits you need from the state, county, or city will depend on your business activities and business location. Your business license fees will also vary.

States tend to regulate a broader range of activities than the federal government. For example, business activities that are commonly regulated locally include auctions, construction, and dry cleaning, farming, plumbing, restaurants, retail, and vending machines.

Some licenses and permits expire after a set period of time. Keep close track of when you need to renew them

— it's often easier to renew than it is to apply for a new one.

You'll have to research your own state, county, and city regulations. Industry requirements often vary by state. Visit your state's website to find out which permits and licenses you need.

Open a business bank account

A small business checking account can help you handle legal, tax, and day-to-day issues. The good news is it's easy to set one up if you have the right registrations and paperwork ready.

Open a business bank account

Open a business account when you're ready to start accepting or spending money as your business. A business bank account helps you stay legally compliant and protected. It also provides benefits to your customers and employees.

Benefits of business bank accounts

As soon as you start accepting or spending money as your business, you should open a business bank account. Common business accounts include a checking account, savings account, credit card account, and a merchant services account. Merchant services accounts allow you to accept credit and debit card transactions from your customers.

You can open a business bank account once you've gotten your federal EIN.

Most business bank accounts offer perks that don't come with a standard personal bank account.

- **Protection**. Business banking offers limited personal liability protection by keeping your business funds separate from your personal funds. Merchant services also offer purchase protection for your customers and ensures that their personal information is secure.
- **Professionalism**. Customers will be able to pay you with credit cards and make checks out to your business instead of directly to you. Plus, you'll be able to authorize employees to handle day-to-day banking tasks on behalf of the business.
- **Preparedness**. Business banking usually comes with the option for a line of credit for the company. This can be used in the event of an emergency, or if your business needs new equipment.
- **Purchasing power**. Credit card accounts can help your business make large startup purchases and help establish a credit history for your business.

Find an account with low fees and good benefits

Some business owners open a business account at the same bank they use for their personal accounts. Rates, fees, and options vary from bank to bank, so you should

shop around to make sure you find the lowest fees and
the best benefits.

Here are things to consider when you're opening a business checking or savings account:

- Introductory offers
- Interest rates for savings and checking
- Interest rates for lines of credit
- Transaction fees
- Early termination fees
- Minimum account balance fees

Here are things to consider when you're opening a merchant services account:

- **Discount rate**: The percentage charged for every transaction processed
- **Transaction fees**: The amount charged for every credit card transaction
- **Address Verification Service (AVS) fees**
- **ACH daily batch fees**: Fees charged when you settle credit card transactions for that day
- **Monthly minimum fees**: Fees charged if your business doesn't meet the minimum required transactions

Payment processing companies are an increasingly popular alternative to traditional merchant services accounts. Payment processing companies sometimes provide extra functionality, like accessories that let you use your phone to accept credit card payments. The fee categories that you need to consider will be similar to merchant services account fees. If you find a payment processor that you like, remember that you'll still need to connect it to a business checking account to receive payments.

- Employer Identification Number (EIN) (or a Social Security number, if you're a sole proprietorship)
- Your business's formation documents
- Ownership agreements
- Business license

Conclusion

Business opportunities are like buses, there's always another one coming. so fasten your belt for success. This book is not only for those in the United States of America but to everyone who understands what is written on it. All you need to do is to check our country's law and follow the instructions listed in this book.

Thank you as you read I still remain your friend and brother Daniel Emesim.

you can connect with me via email at danielemesim06@yahoo.com

and please make sure you follow me on Facebook because I post content of great value there.

https://www.facebook.com/daniel.emesim.7